Set Pieces

Ted Pearson

Spuyten Duyvil
New York City

"Incidentals" 1-4 first appeared in *Three Fold*.

©2021 by Ted Pearson
ISBN 978-1-956005-10-3
Cover: Theo van Doesburg, *Komposition XIII*, 1918

All rights reserved.

Library of Congress Cataloging-in-Publication Data

Names: Pearson, Ted, author.
Title: Set pieces / Ted Pearson.
Description: New York City : Spuyten Duyvil, [2021] |
Identifiers: LCCN 2021033144 | ISBN 9781956005103 (paperback)
Subjects: LCGFT: Poetry.
Classification: LCC PS3566.E2353 S48 2021 | DDC 811/.54--dc23
LC record available at https://lccn.loc.gov/2021033144

In Memory of Jackson Mac Low

A set is a Many that allows itself to be thought of as a One.
Georg Cantor

Contents

Down & Across   1

Incidentals   15

Conditional Release   23

Vacant Premises   37

Tesseract   45

Subject to Doubt   59

No Vacancy   65

Stolen Moments   71

Fire Music   85

Equinox   93

Codices   107

Matchsticks   115

Down & Across

1.

Introvert life is benchmarked by defeats.
The odds on beating the house are nil.

It's hard to survive your expectations when
Language affords you no shelter to speak of.

Right angles mock your perpetual drift.
Miracles speak to your sense of the absurd.

The culture police have closed the borders.
Who will mourn the wild child's fate?

We have come to the end of another era.
Alexa! Use meretricious in a sentence.

While the search goes on for your lost libido,
Your memory essays your reckless past.

2.

Lust isn't love, but it has its charms,
As lovers attest in each other's arms.

What can't be named will not be tamed.
The oracles agree. It's all in your head.

Twilight finds you lost in the pharmakon.
Let's count the ways to hit bottom.

Your morning labors leave you spent,
But "surely, the tide comes in twice a day."

Obvious to remark, we are mostly water.
Childhood's mandate was sink or swim.

Let there be no talk of resurrection.
Each next poem might be your last.

3.

The *pass* completes your formal education.
You have wrapped your troubles in dreams.

The sanctuary opens on a stairway to the stars.
From there, it's only seven steps to heaven.

As the last in a series of historical asides,
Nothing comes of standing by your word.

The current regime has silenced your song
With anthems of blood and soil.

By factors so vast you seek an abridgement,
The City of Ciphers explodes into view.

Then you descend and resume your life
Among people "incapable of contact."

4.

With the casual grace of a practiced dancer,
You tender your mercies and your resignation.

Once you've gathered your bushel of doubt,
To be quit with offers a kind of consolation.

In a life spent milking blood from a stone,
Your blind side faces wherever you turn.

When totality beckons, fangs and all,
You barely escape The Big Picture.

Chalk it up to a bad case of nerves. You live
In the shadow of the sum of your parts.

But as long as the Grail remains at large,
Its legend will secure your existence.

5.

Subjects flow from the subject factory.
Desire spirals from disaster to disaster.

Where life exacts a succession of failures,
Reality appears as a kind of delirium.

Evidence of thought is missing in action.
Chronic fantasies supplant your dreams.

Fantasies of place, in which you have one.
Fantasies of time, in which you survive.

Exiled, you pass through uncharted waters.
At sunset, you turn your back on the sea.

Sleep evades you, but not these voices,
Which linger like uninvited guests.

6.

"The object *is*. Now what objects *aren't*?"
Do we write just to fill these pages?

Other voices tell other lies. Finding yourself
At a loss for words should come as no surprise.

Dead silence greeted your latest recital.
Heartbreak followed you into the street.

When heavy weather approached the city,
Rolling thunder wasn't far behind.

Imaginary lightning illumines your path
As if you were not (and are not) alone.

The object in question speaks for itself.
You speak at peril if you speak at all.

7.

Introvert life is benchmarked by defeats.
The odds on beating the house are nil.

Lust isn't love, but it has its charms,
As lovers attest in each others' arms.

The *pass* completes your formal education.
You have wrapped your troubles in dreams.

Subjects flow from the subject factory.
Desire spirals from disaster to disaster.

With the casual grace of a practiced dancer,
You tender your mercies and your resignation.

"The object *is*. Now what objects *aren't?*"
Do we write just to fill these pages?

8.

It's hard to survive your expectations when
Language affords you no shelter to speak of.

What can't be named will not be tamed.
The oracles agree. It's all in your head.

The sanctuary opens on a stairway to the stars.
From there, it's only seven steps to heaven.

Once you've gathered your bushel of doubts,
To be quit with offers a kind of consolation.

Where life exacts a succession of failures,
Reality appears as a kind of delirium.

Other voices tell other lies. Finding yourself
At a loss for words should come as no surprise.

9.

Miracles appeal to your sense of the absurd.
Right angles mock your perpetual drift.

At twilight, you're lost in the pharmakon.
Let's count the ways you could hit bottom.

As the last in a series of historical asides,
Nothing comes of standing by your word.

In a life spent milking blood from a stone,
Your blind side faces wherever you turn.

Evidence of thought is missing in action.
Chronic fantasies supplant your dreams.

When heavy weather approaches the city,
Rolling thunder is closer than it seems.

10.

The culture police have closed the border.
Who will mourn the wild child's fate?

Your morning labors leave you spent.
But "surely, the tide comes in twice a day."

The current regime has stilled your song
With anthems of blood and soil.

Dead silence greeted your latest recital.
Heartbreak followed you into the street.

When totality beckoned, fangs and all,
You barely escaped The Big Picture –

From fantasies of place, in which you have one,
To fantasies of time, in which you survive.

11.

We have come to the end of another era.
Alexa! Use meretricious in a sentence.

Obvious to remark, we are mostly water.
Childhood's mandate was sink or swim.

By factors so vast you seek an abridgement,
The City of Ciphers explodes into view.

Chalk it up to a bad case of nerves. You live
In the shadow of the sum of your parts.

Exiled, you pass through uncharted waters.
At sunset, you turn your back on the sea.

Imaginary lightning illumines your path
As if you were not (and are not) alone.

12.

While the search goes on for your lost libido,
Your memory essays your reckless past.

Let there be no talk of resurrection.
Each next poem might be your last.

Then you rally and resume your life
Among people "incapable of contact."

As long as the Grail remains at large,
Its legend will secure your existence.

Sleep evades you, but not these voices
That linger like uninvited guests.

The object in question speaks for itself.
You speak at peril if you speak at all.

Incidentals

1.

With few tools and scant know-how, we are building a movement to resist the forces that have made us what we are. Ideology functions by remote control, which is how it dictates the psychic economy that rules our damaged lives. The lumpen dignify their abjection by aiding and abetting the rule of the oligarchs. All that we, in a word, reject as the bane of our works and days. Even as our nights are ours alone, they are no less bound by regulations, no less subject to surveillance. Whence, the attempts to gaslight the pain that accompanies our historical condition. Which must be acknowledged, even as we seek a world devoid of unnecessary suffering. Such is the famously utopian premise that warrants our posing the old conundrum: what is to be done? *That* is the question that, not for nothing, now belongs to you.

2.

Imagine a chorus of self-ordained poets, as if there were any other kind. Nobody knows the trouble they've seen because "no one listens to poetry." Imagine their voices swelling in defiance as they march in lockstep down the boulevard of dreams. *Marketing the gift. Marketing the gift. They shall come rejoicing, marketing the gift.* Nor will they have gained the world thereby, though that was once on offer. Instead, they find themselves utterly seduced by the myth of the one true self. The one they imagine is uniquely theirs, if only because they think so. If poetry favors those who want it, it's clearly not for everyone. You can just ask around, if you don't believe me, but know that the answer will be bad for morale. In fact, it will only add to the pain that you've already brought to the table.

3.

Between sheltering in place and assuming the position comes our unrequited love of justice. Unless, of course, you have no place and therefore have no shelter. Displays of privilege are de rigueur where water nymphs lounge by infinity pools and gossip about their clients. The nymphs will concede that they're paid to be bored. Thus emerges a political economy disguised as a Venus flytrap. Ask your mother regarding nectar as a medium of exchange. Toxic discourse sets the stage where global conflicts rage. A continent is burning, sad to say, but such are the stakes in the war against nature. Indeed, it's the selfsame masters of war who have turned the culture of mayhem to account. In their world, violence is healthy competition under cover of a smoke-filled sky. Meanwhile, back at the infinity pool, Orpheus plays his final set while DNA is exchanged.

4.

What of life in the mighty miasma (the great dismal swamp) (the imperial city) where the word of the day is *cockroach*? Bravado masks the people's fears as if they were bred for the trenches. This brings joy to the privateers whose black sites hide under bouncy houses and whose evil knows no bounds. Meanwhile, the myth of the Zeitgeist will persist for as long as you believe in ghosts. There are only tenors in search of vehicles. There are only parasites in search of hosts. Population flows follow well-known trade routes. With record numbers of refugees, the fires of their encampments are visible from space. Anxious asylum seekers crowd ports of call in flight from the Law of the Father. Where rockets make for hard rain, mass graves open below the fold. When national interests are aligned with capital, widespread poverty follows.

5.

Identity is strictly epiphenomenal. Our only foundation is the ground we walk on, which in these parts is far from stable. For as much as you remain a puzzle to yourself, the pieces remain the same. Well adapted to the status quo. Perfectly interchangeable. Ready to scale up or down at a glance and to replicate themselves to infinity. The myth of equality masks your plight. Your dreams are reflected in a broken mirror, even as autonomy hums in the tain. The last gods standing are Wealth and Power, and only their favored creditors will be welcome to share the spoils. When they punch your ticket to the Gravediggers' Ball, you'll get your dance with the Devil. Meanwhile, we fight over table scraps and endure the funereal tenor of our days. Between the bullet and the ballot box, it's time to pick your poison.

6.

You wake to a landscape rife with grammar whose exercise fills you with remorse. Your daybook is littered with infinite digressions. Your night sweats testify against your dreams. Resistance requires a measure of freedom, from which a politics emerges. The oracle has spoken. It's all in your head. But justice withheld is justice denied. And forbearance can resemble complicity. Though force will not provide the form, form itself is a force to be reckoned with. You long to caress a body of knowledge that can point toward a better future. A life's work secures the work of a lifetime. Not, as it happens, an identity. To rehearse a language into the night is to yearn for new horizons. Words point to the thing itself. "A living mind, and that one's own." With which we dissect the lies that have passed too long for discourse.

7.

With few tools and scant knowhow, we are building a movement to resist the forces that have made us into what we are. Imagine a chorus of self-ordained poets, as if there were any other kind. Between sheltering in place and assuming the position comes our unrequited love of justice. What then of life in the mighty miasma (the dismal swamp) (the imperial city) where the word of the day is *cockroach*? Identity is strictly epiphenomenal. You wake to a landscape rife with grammar, whose exercise fills you with remorse. Ideology functions by remote control; whence, it dictates the psychic economy that rules our damaged lives. Nobody knows the trouble we've seen because "no one listens to poetry." And what of those who have no place and therefore have no shelter? Bravado masks the people's fears as if they were bred for the trenches.

8.

Our only foundation is the ground we walk on, which in these parts is far from stable. Your daybook is littered with infinite digressions. The lumpen barely survive immiseration, and still they stand with the oligarchs. Imagine their voices swelling in defiance as they march in lock-step down the boulevard of dreams. To assume the position would be ill-advised. It could only bring joy to the privateers whose black sites hide under bouncy houses and whose evil knows no bounds. For as much as you remain a puzzle to yourself, the missing pieces are all the same. Your night sweats testify against your dreams. All that we, in a word, reject. All that's the bane of our works and days. *Marketing the gift. Marketing the gift. They shall come rejoicing, marketing the gift.* Meanwhile, at the infinity pool, nymphs prattle on about their clients.

9.

Be assured that the myth of the Zeitgeist will persist as long as you believe in ghosts. Perfectly attuned to the daily grind, resistance requires a measure of freedom for a politics to emerge. And, while our nights are supposedly our own, they are no less bound by regulations, no less subject to surveillance. Nor will we gain the world thereby, though that was once on offer. The nymphs admit they're paid to be bored. While tenors go in search of vehicles, parasites go in search of hosts. They are perfectly interchangeable. Ever ready to scale up or down. And more than willing to replicate to infinity. The oracle has spoken. I am not a pronoun. Although we attempt to counter those who would gaslight the pain of our historical condition, many find themselves utterly seduced by the myth of the one true self.

10.

Thus, there emerges a political economy disguised as a Venus flytrap. Population flows follow known trade routes. The myth of equality masks your plight. But justice withheld is justice denied. Which must be acknowledged, even as we seek a world devoid of unnecessary suffering. A world that we imagine uniquely ours, if only because we think so. Regarding nectar as a medium of exchange, look to your sainted mother. With record numbers of refugees, the fires of their encampments are visible from space. Their last known dreams were broken promises. Even as forbearance mirrored complicity, thoughts of autonomy hummed in the tain. Such is the famously utopian premise that warrants our posing the old conundrum: what is to be done? Poetry favors those who want it, but it's clearly not for everyone. Long nights follow our endless days, and so the struggle continues.

11.

Continents are burning, sad to say, but such are the stakes in the war against nature. Asylum seekers crowd ports of call in flight from the Law of the Father. The last gods standing are Wealth and Power, and only their creditors will share in the spoils. While force will not provide the form, form itself is a force to be reckoned with. *That* is the challenge that, not for nothing, now belongs to you. Just ask around, if you don't believe me, but know that the answer will be bad for morale. The masters of war stay true to form. They are pleased to embrace the culture of mayhem, which in their world means healthy competition. Wherever rockets make hard rain, mass graves open below the fold. When they punch your ticket to the Gravediggers' Ball, you'll get your dance with the Devil.

12.

You long to caress a body of knowledge that can point toward a better future. In fact, it will only add to the pain that you've already brought to the table. Meanwhile, back at the infinity pool, Orpheus plays his final set while DNA is exchanged. When national interests align with capital, widespread poverty follows. Whence, under cover of smoke-filled skies, we fight each other over table scraps and endure the funereal tenor of our days. A life's work signifies the work of a lifetime. Not, as it happens, an identity. Between the bullet and the ballot box, you're free to pick your poison. To rehearse a language into the night is to yearn for new horizons. Signs point to the thing itself. "A living mind, and that one's own." With which you dissect the countless lies that have passed too long for discourse.

Conditional Release

1.

Every closure

        is also an opening.

      Victory is certain,

           if also Pyrrhic.

      The shroud gapes

           that also drapes.

      Prophecy reveals

              what it conceals.

"The oracle neither

      speaks nor hides,"

    but riddles us a future

        that is all too present,

     all too certain,

          and Pyrrhic.

2.

Visible effects

    define an action.

"I is an instance

    of saying I."

  What does it mean

    to be *connected*

  if not by our works

    and days?

We seek the truth

  of what we know.

  Not in the act,

    but in the visible

  effects of truth's

    historic destitution.

3.

Between the zenith

        of thought and the

      nadir of suffering –

          "the two sides of

        noon and the two

               sides of midnight" –

          the subject lives in

                 exile from itself.

Despite the voices

        that ride the wind,

     it is lonely here

          in the absence of

      others, who also

            think and suffer.

4.

The blank page

    is a metonym

        for "the white sail

            of our unconcern,"

      itself a metonym

               for the ship of fools

            that foundered on the

                    shoals of mastery.

Old School dreams

        of autonomy

    aside, our true

           legacy remains

      an enigma, lost in

              an empire of signs.

5.

A difficult dilemma

        defines our plight

    at the crossroads

        where theory

     and practice

         intersect and

      thought concedes

           the unthinkable.

The glow of

    hellfire confirms

our suspicions.

      There is no

    turning back

        from the light.

6.

Life is an epistemic

        adventure. Thought

    is a only a matter

          of time. The poem

              is something more

        and other than it

                presumes to say.

The oracle calls for

        Death to Tyrants!

    while freedom songs

          indict the State,

     which foments fear

           and fosters hate.

7.

Every closure

        is also an opening.

    Each next line is

        a throw of the dice.

    The pen "neither

        speaks nor hides

    its meaning." The shape

        of art abides.

Ghost language

        (it says right here)

    is not to be avoided.

        Other lines say other-

    wise. They speak, if

        at all, in tongues.

8.

Visible effects

        define an action.

    Song defies the

        bounds of time.

      Even as it hides

         a fiction, truth

      resides *within*

             each rhyme.

Not for nothing

      have we come this

    far. Where precarity

      leads to struggle,

    we are more than

        they say we are.

9.

Between the zenith

        of thought and

    and the elisions

          of dreams,

      the subject wrestles

              with constraints.

          Love without pain

                remains untested.

Pain without purpose

      remains to be endured.

    Even so, your dreams

         protest, you'll

     miss us when

          we're gone.

10.

The blank page

        is a metonym

    for the blinding

           light of sunrise.

        The poet wakes to

              a world of words

           where nothing is

                    lost in translation.

Bygone dreams

        of freedom return

     as the poem emerges,

          line by line. They

      say "it takes

              a worried mind..."

11.

A difficult dilemma

        defines a plight.

What some call praxis,

        we call work –

the work we do,

        the work that does,

    and the work that

           remains to be done.

The composer arranges

    words to be sung.

  All it takes to parse

      what he's done

  is an open mind and

        a willing tongue.

12.

Life is an epistemic

    adventure. Mental

        projections (actual

            size) in reality

        come to nought.

                Virtue proclaimed is

            virtue denied unless

                    it leads to thought.

We, whose rulers are

        clowns and bullies,

      seek to hasten their

            demise. Failing which,

    we'll meet our fate: death

                by a thousand lies.

Vacant Premises

1.

Imagine a mountain that remains a mountain, no matter how long you sit here. Spectrum analysis of love's true colors reveals a motley of bruises. If that's tough love, include me out. Even now, you scribble at your peril. The music of a lifetime is slipping away. Over drinks, a prospective suicide admits to being a perpetual beginner. Anxiety is that which doesn't deceive. Logic ratifies the terms of your estrangement. To confirm, you were together, and then you were not. Why do we call some angles sharp? What exactly makes circles round? Mind your matter is sound advice. We have no need of the thoughts and prayers or the moral judgments of morons. What we need are feet on the street to ensure that the struggle continues.

2.

News is war by other means, and truth is its very first victim. Ghosts rage at the options on offer. Puppets lobby for a place at the table without any strings attached. Necessity may be your only luxury. Your absent other is your better self. Proof resides in your empty mirror. Reality decays at a precise rate. Eros Absconditus is the god of the moment. We sleep; we work; we are numb to desire. Dreams of past lives pass in review. Your "errors and wrecks" defy analysis. The presumption of innocence is simply that. The dead are collateral damage. There's a calculus of characters embedded in language, a collocation of winks and nods. Everything flows from their shapes and sounds. Broken spirits rise after dark and slowly make their rounds.

3.

As a social construct, the People are an effect of wealth and power. Ruins stand as the artifacts of empire. When things fall apart, where do they land? The parsimony principle clearly states that without you, I am no one. Poetics emphasizes temporal bonds. Ethics organizes spatial relations. There's a liminal world between sleep and forgetting. If infinite monkeys can rewrite Shakespeare, a toy poodle could type this line. This is called the will to power, specifically the power of words. To be swaddled in righteousness is but one example. It's hard to finesse an internal collapse. Exultant rage is the death of tyranny. This is known as burning down the house. Thus spoke the oracle: do the math. We are more than they say we are.

4.

The tradition of "number, weight, and measure" is lost in infinite flux. Spoken words parody the common tongue. The public sphere is tarnished by degraded discourse. To which the People have pledged their troth. In which the power of the mob resides. With nothing to show for decades of rhetoric, curses rain on market day. Austerity must choose between bread and circuses. Imperial melancholy seeks relief. Our new anthem is Send In the Clowns. Recognition follows pitch discrimination. A monody is a melody at one with its constraints. Bright moments interrupt years of drudgery. A world's age approaches completion. The stars alone secure your fate. In the present climate, principled dissent can lead to social death.

5.

Every ideal degenerates into another perjured reality. Political forms are inherently unstable. Poetic forms are manifest dreams. What can't be sutured leaves a hole in the fabric, replete with imaginary numbers. To clarify the thoughts to which our signifiers cling, we invoke their names, which remain legible even when under erasure. From knots to splices to somber redactions, our entanglements underwrite wordless particulars. Pushback comes from the pushback poem, its words lately sprung from the matrix of surds. How will we know when the future arrives? The perceiving subject, not to be dismissed, balks when confronted by bare life. Where movements are prone to dissolution, institutions are subject to decay.

6.

Starting over was never an option. The rebellion begins with you. Learning advances through the knowledge of particulars. Things present themselves, word for word. The days of the present ignominy are numbered. Shrouded effigies hang from lamp posts. Weather reports spread disinformation. The new anarchy abjures cocktails in favor of pulling at the empire's threads. Deferred maintenance leads to loss of liberty. It's the phoenix that rises from the ashes, not the eagle. We must cure the nation of imperial ambition. We must root out the fascists, one and all. Despite the best efforts of the one percent, the experiment is not yet over. It remains to be seen whether Plato was right. Must democracy end in tyranny?

7.

What we need are feet on the street to ensure that the struggle continues. We have no need of the thoughts and prayers or the moral judgment of morons. Mind your matter is sound advice. Why do we call some angles sharp? What exactly makes circles round? To confirm, you were together, and then you were not. Logic ratifies the terms of your estrangement. Anxiety is that which doesn't deceive. Over cocktails, the prospective suicide admits to being a perpetual beginner. The music of a lifetime is slipping away. Even now, you scribble at your peril. Spectral analysis of love's true colors reveals a motley of bruises. If that's tough love, include me out. Imagine a mountain that remains a mountain, no matter how long you sit here.

8.

Broken spirits arise out of nowhere and slowly begin their rounds. There's a calculus of characters embedded in language, a collocation of winks and nods. Everything flows from their shapes and sounds. The presumption of innocence is simply that. Even as the dead are collateral damage, your "errors and wrecks" defy analysis. Dreams of past lives pass in review. We sleep; we work; we are numb to desire. Eros Absconditus is the god of the moment. Reality decays at a precise rate. Proof resides in your empty mirror. Necessity may be your only luxury. Your absent other is your better self. Puppets lobby for a place at the table without any strings attached. Ghosts rage at the options on offer. News is war by other means, and truth is its very first victim.

9.

We are more and other than they say we are. Thus spoke the oracle: do the math. Exultant rage is the death of tyranny. This is known as burning down the house. It's hard to finesse an internal collapse. To be swaddled in righteousness is but one example. This follows from the will to power, specifically the power of words. If infinite monkeys can rewrite Shakespeare, a toy poodle could type this line. There's a liminal world between sleep and forgetting. Ethics organizes spatial relations. Poetics emphasizes temporal bonds. When things fall apart, where do they land? The parsimony principle clearly states that without you, I am no one. Ruins stand as the artifacts of empire. As a social construct, the People just are an effect of wealth and power.

10.

In the present climate, principled dissent can lead to social death. The stars alone can secure your fate. Bright moments interrupt patterns of judgment. Actions are defined by opposite reactions. Even as one thing follows another, melody relies on discrimination. Whence, this monody based, as it is, on systems of constraint. Our new anthem is Send In the Clowns. Imperial melancholy seeks relief. Austerity must choose between bread and circuses. With nothing to show for decades of rhetoric, curses rain on market day. In which the power of the mob resides. To which the People have pledged their troth. The public sphere is tarnished by degraded discourse. Spoken words parody the common tongue. The tradition of "number, weight, and measure" is lost in infinite flux.

11.

Where movements are prone to dissolution, institutions are subject to decay. The perceiving subject, not to be dismissed, balks when confronted by bare life. How will we know when the future arrives? Pushback comes from the pushback poem, which began in a matrix of surds. From knots and splices to somber redactions, our entanglements underwrite wordless particulars. To clarify the thoughts to which signifiers cling, we invoke their names, which remain legible, even when under erasure. What can't be sutured leaves a hole in the fabric to be filled with imaginary numbers. Poetic forms are manifest dreams. Political forms are inherently unstable. Sooner or later, our ideals will degrade into yet another perjured reality.

12.

It remains to be seen whether Plato was right. Must democracies end in tyranny? Despite the best efforts of the one percent, the experiment isn't over. We must root out the fascists, one and all, and with them their imperial ambitions. It's the phoenix that rises from the ashes, not the eagle. Deferred maintenance leads to loss of liberty. The new anarchy abjures cocktails, preferring to pull at the empire's threads. Weather reports spread disinformation. If and how become where and when. The days of the present ignominy are numbered. Shrouded effigies hang from lamp posts. Learning advances through knowledge of particulars. Things present themselves, word for word. Starting over was never an option. The rebellion begins with you.

Tesseract

1.

Fictive depths suborn
        the plot to expose their
                credible illusions. The self

is a composite of mixed
        motives; none amount
                to a sufficient cause.

Chance reigns between
        the State's exhibits and its
                efforts to prove a negative.

There's a void in politics
        that language can't fill,
                a lack of significant content.

There are those who learn
        to survive their beliefs and those
                who can't live without them.

And then there's that hint
        of misdirection to prolong
                our pursuit of the Grail.

2.

No truth is self evident.
        The myth of an original
                unity of being is a sop

to adepts with duct tape.
        But all the king's horses
                and all the king's men.

But what price bananas?
        And who has the time?
                Let there be no talk of

restoration – of a past
        that never was. Instead,
                let's talk of reparations

in the name of the dis-
        possessed. Tack *those* on
                to the national debt.

Bananas are selling six
        for a dollar. The State
                is in dire disrepair.

3.

Paradigms put up conceptual
        roadblocks. Where A equals
                A, A also equals A.

It's a matter of doubling, not
        of doubting. Of reciprocity,
                if not solidarity.

And, as we've taken pains to
        explain, our readers refuse
                to be silent witnesses.

It is they who must overcome
        the myth of transparency.
                They for whom

the most gnomic phrases
        are the opening gambits in
                the invention of truth.

There lie the tensions between
        our intentions and the words
                that appear on the page.

4.

Actions are based on
    the knowledge they affirm
        whenever it's acted upon.

An epochal change – in
    kind, not degree – submits
        to a present that has taken

its place in the long view
    to which history aspires
        and in which it seeks

its end. Which is not ours,
    though our day will come.
        But, until it does, there are

poems to glean. What
    remains to be done
        remains to be seen.

The truth of this question,
    which is not one, resides
        in its bold iterations.

5.

The letter of the text is a
    symptom of the conflict in
        which meaning functions

as a free radical and truth
    is reduced to begging for
        scraps from the last oracle

in town. These serve as
    warnings against assimilation.
        Beware the perils that

define a landscape of arid
    mountains, impassable deserts,
        and broken sun-bleached

bones. A desolate landscape
    that's inhospitable to all who
        would traverse it. To all,

that is, in thrall to the
    Sublime and the mythic
        allure of the Grail.

6.

Composition absolves chaos
    of any predatory intent.
        If it says anything

worth hearing, even though it
    elude our understanding,
        poetry can't be consigned

to the warehouse where
    history stores its dates and
        claims. Where telling

your truth wins out over
    discourse, the telling becomes
        another discourse. And

what it says is "real." This isn't
    the time or place to debate
        the causes behind this

illusion. What concerns us
    now are the consequences
        to which we here submit.

7.

What kind of love is at
        the heart of thought if not
                the love of what can't be

known? Does the act of
        knowing then presuppose
                a point of no return?

The tragic sense of life
        is based on the knowledge
                that nothing escapes

inexistence. No way around
        these systems of constraints. No
                higher purpose than pure

impossibility. Of thought
        in the meanwhile. Of life
                in the end. In theory,

the choice is equal to
        the act when the
                act is an act of love.

8.

    As the State formation
        approaches endgame,
            capital strips its re-

maining assets while its citizens
    dwell in a world on the brink
        and wait for the final collapse.

Sad to say, they are not
    wrong. The State has
        sold them out for a song.

Thereby bringing wealth
    and dishonor to scions
        in the Name of the Father.

Who rightly fear the growing
    unrest in a nation where
        abject misery attests

that the State has failed to
    protect its people and that father
        rarely knows best.

9.

Vengeance will arrive
        on an bitter wind, but it's no
                less welcome for that. It was

just such a wind that brought
        us to this moment, and
                it hasn't died down yet.

In the lunatic light of the
        daily grind, the Lords of
                Misrule resemble the living

dead who comprise their
        base. Of whom it's been
                said they're no better than

they should be. In fact,
        they are very much worse.
                As profiteers mark up their

daily fare, the people dwell
        in misery which they lack
                the political will to repair.

10.

Poetry composes the silence
        in his head. Caesurae mark
                where the dead have spoken.

Language is a system of dis-
        crepant sounds. Without a
                lexicon, it's pure music.

These few lines are acts of
        desire; they call forth
                the will to surrender.

The future of meaning is
        on the horizon, where
                truth's multiplicity abides.

In fact, though it was his truth
        to tell, he wondered what
                the words he'd been given

would say. And what his readers
        might take away from within
               the surrounding silence.

11.

The future manifests hard
    use and dreary habitations.
        Walled cities built of

regimented stones over-
    look the Plain of Precarity.
        Makeshift slums house

the mad king's subjects.
    The only weather is cata-
        strophic. And the only

outlook dire. Such is the
    setting of the tales we were
        told of how we came to

be here – in the dark
    pauses, the interstitial
        moonlight – where here

is a fantasy that, after
    we're gone, these songs
        will sing themselves.

12.

Where language is mostly
      mental noise, writing is
           mere transcription. This

we designate ghost language.
      Proof, if needed, that the
           dead are with us still.

That against all odds, we are
      not alone, though the rooms
           are silent and the house

is dark. Proof, if needed, that
      their words are in our heads.
           Words they say they were

desperate to write, which is
      famously what one says.
           There's a world of words,

and it's yours for the taking,
      even if, as the ghosts insist, it
           leads to your unmaking.

Subject to Doubt

1.

Dead reckoning allows for drift, which accounts for our wayward claims. While evidence of thought is missing in action, traces of last night's warmth still linger, as do fragments of last night's dream. Daylight breaks on sole survivors. Fugitive flesh awakes.

2.

Totality emerges, fangs and all. Identities traverse the Euclidian distance. Even as their losses decimate their ranks, capital's conscripts aim for the summit. Thus is it said, "The descent follows . . . endless and indestructible."

3.

With few tools and scant know-how, we greeted the temptation to exist. Religion sacralized the search for meaning though we dressed the part at our peril. Later delusions died in previews. Whence they assigned us spirit-guides to ease our next transition.

4.

For as much as you remain a puzzle to yourself, no one discourse will explain you away. Whatever you said is what we heard, regardless of what you meant. Variant endings must have their day lest your narrative get in the way.

5.

The oracle neither speaks nor hides. Hence, the power of unshared secrets to stymie unabashed desires. Though life is a motley of ill-advised choices, the young are encouraged to find their voices. Further follies will surely follow. Along the yellow brick road.

6.

Hard-won fluencies fall by the wayside. Thought is only a matter of time. Common sense basks in noonday light, the very apex of vacuity. Then comes the long glissade into twilight. Then darkness. Then nothing. Subject to doubt, "can these bones live?"

7.

Institutions are subject to decay, but a nation is not a theme park. Neither will the margins of the poem provide a viable habitat for lovers. Even when you're at home in your body, isn't estrangement the very type of the subject's relation to itself?

8.

Principled dissent courts social death, but fallen angels tend to land on their feet. Personal pronouns are damaged goods, subject to time and rumors. You'll find them in a roadhouse on the outskirts of hell, where they drink to kingdom come.

9.

History aspires to predictive eminence. In fact, it's a morgue for lost causes, grotesque fictions, and odd plots. How tell the one from all the rest? Taking the long view avails us not, who dwell on borrowed time.

10.

Composition absolves chaos of any predatory intent. A fading star does a slow burn as it tries to adapt to diminished resources. Though dreams of distinction inspire these songs, the Annals insist that opposites attract. That life and death are one.

11.

His humor was darkest while he was in mourning. That's what it means to be dialed in. At first, we figured it was his way of grieving. Instead, it was his prelude to leaving. Seeking freedom from mental chains. Half-forgotten faces. Half-remembered names.

12.

Memories resonate. Then, they die. And perhaps it would be better if we died with them. All for one leaves none for all. Absent any discernible aura, your ghostly presence casts a pall. What kind of future did you expect with a past beyond recall?

No Vacancy

1.

We're approaching precisely the point we were making – the point of no return. There are destinies yet to be played out and parallels yet to be drawn. Where memories linger, scars remain. Form and function share a fatal attraction from opposite sides of the tain.

2.

Do you suppose your actions constitute a self? Do you suppose that warrants your existence? Policy requires you to disappear. We call this auto-assimilation. In due course, there will be no traces. Then, you'll be one of us.

3.

Rejection is integral to natural selection. And it frees you from the sepulcher of hope. The first-born Fate was bred for her inapposite views. The middle one was keen on first principles. To the youngest it fell to express their regret for the losses you're about to incur.

4.

The shortest distance between two sentences is the time it takes to serve one. No one can do your time but you. It's called hard labor for good reason. It's among the most corporeal of virtues, but it will not set you free.

5.

We drew distinctions on the walls of the cave. Fanciful figures caught the spirit of the hunt. Sacrificial beasts fed the guests and then some. Such were the origins of genre painting in the days between feast and famine.

6.

Language is much too dark to see through, yet truth is said to illumine speech. Trauma leads to arrested development. Confession is said to be good for the soul. Style takes the measure of a life between thoughts – and to this day no one the wiser.

7.

Abstraction overwrote the status quo. Mnemonic traces tell the tale. Cell death, being a subtractive process, is closely aligned with modern art. Redaction is one of its critical phases. Only then does the stone come alive, complete with missing parts.

8.

For whom does poetry remain an option? By which we mean the act itself, which constitutes its matter. Also known as unending desire, its words – "and let the writing be of words" – are the signal fires of futurity.

9.

Short-term memories flicker and fade. Taking the long view avails us not. Where the middle voice favors intimations, between plain speech and wordless song, a text emerges from the silence that surrounds us. "As if all worlds were there."

10.

Fallen angels tend to land on their feet. Ever ready, for the price of a pint, to recount the highlights of their journey here, which they call Hell on Earth. That's what we've made of what we were given. And with no better place to be.

11.

Imaginary numbers shape the sum of our desires. Mortal thoughts keep our feet to the fire. Our chances at heaven have grown remote. So we place our trust in the fecund Void of which Lu Chi once wrote.

12.

The war against nature has defiled the planet. Other wars decimate the ranks of the poor. Statecraft is nought but a kind of stagecraft. The elite can always do less with more. But the scale of our losses has grown since then to include our metaphors.

Stolen Moments

1.

A deep shine adds a new
        dimension to the mirror in
                which you talk to yourself.

The resulting transcript
        must then find a cadence
                to measure the music in

your words. And, even then,
        a slow hand is needed to
                coax them onto the page.

On the evidence, few have
        the patience to endure
                their mortality with grace.

Witness this series of
        divagations, each one subject
                to interpellation.

None of which can allay
        our fear that the end of our
                works and days draws near.

2.

Place names cue your
    memories of place, albeit
        there's nobody home.

On the one hand, "I
    wanted to write a poem."
        On the other, the slopes

of Parnassus. In the world
    of difference (I love and I
        hate) one is but one

of many. Our memories
    are oases on the highway
        to oblivion.

Our higher calling is to "fail
    better" because failure is
        endemic to the art.

Loss leads to longing, a
    sign of lack. The Orphic
        error was looking back.

3.

Bold schematics gloss
        the forebrain. Fossilized
                odes, recumbent in amber,

remind us of our youth.
        Chance takes a knee when
                fools rush in. The inmates

riot when school lets out.
        Old habits form lasting
                patterns. Needle tracks

lead to the Land of Nod.
        Trolley tracks run past the
                poetry store. Low-flying

lizards rattle a populace
        long since accustomed
                to death from above.

Broken stanzas expose
        themselves to rumor
                and further research.

4.

    Posterity began with a
        standing start. Ghostly
            transmissions haunted

    the airwaves. The great
        dead reckoned on some-
            where to be. Free-range

    verses traced a circuit.
        Sideshows trafficked in
            petrodollars. Sophists

    tendered smoke and
        mirrors to neophytes
            raised on suspect certainties.

    The master's catalog languished
        in a vitrine. The tallow of
            tradition was easily rendered.

    Less so the tally of feral
        phonemes, whose thrum
            is the hum of poetry.

5.

Bold headers wedded to a
        common cause say meaning
                varies by definition. What

do these signifiers stand
        for in reality? What does reality
                stand for in the brain?

Stunted formations obscure
        their context. Blunt-force
                ballads are not for the faint.

Mister Bones, a statutory
        drunk, was nicely attired
                for the Day of the Dead.

Songs of attrition on
        the road to perdition
                echoed in his head.

Born and raised under
        cover of darkness, all
                he heard is all he said.

6.

A destination is not a thing,
        no matter you say we must
                have one. Thus, we began

our pilgrimage with meager
        rations and false starts. Pro-
                crastination is not a virtue,

although you'd beg to defer.
        Though many pilgrims have
                trod this path, in memory

of their desires, the odds on
        an epic ending are slim.
                Where seasoned tropes

are ready to rumble,
        the truth you seek can
                only abstain.

The brain in pain is
        barely sane, is it all that
                strange to wonder why?

7.

Tomorrow and tomorrow,
        we'll take stock. It's become
                a habit with us.

Whose Dulcinea was Our
        Lady of Sorrows now
                oversees our habitus.

Have you ever noticed
        that chance and justice are
                rumored to be blind? Or

that almost any job
        amounts to buying or
                selling time? Try as we

might to escape our memories,
        where would we be
                without them? We pose these

questions, which remain open,
        because we are well and truly lost,
                even to ourselves.

8.

Sing a song of sufferance.
    Your damaged pride be
        damned! Thus, the geezer,

live from Geezerville. Who
    could but wish that his com-
        patriots were wise. Yes, indeed.

It's simply dynastic, how one
    fool directly follows another in
        the ranks of the generations.

Heroes all, no doubt. But
    we're not here to praise. The
        big disaster said everything

must go! Overeager wings
    wandered too near the sun. This
        changed how we deployed

our forces, including the
    Phantom of the Fleeting Presence –
        strictly hail and farewell.

9.

The clown effect provoked
        some hysteria. An artifact
                of childhood sexual abuse.

Deep in the shadows, life
        goes on. Even as the poem,
                addressed to shadows,

chronicles the culture's
        descent into madness.
                What twisted loyalty

repeats the fathers' sins?
        The poet of childhood must
                tarry with the negative.

That's where the truth of
        the genre resides. That's
                why we call it giving

up the ghost. How else
        see what it is to be what
                it says it is and does?

10.

Whenever a moot point
        stymies your advance,
                revisit your passion

for burned bridges. Wherever
        head tones breach the code,
                a hack is approaching

a brink. Subtle noises,
        the size of a poem, echo at
                length in a widening gyre.

The air is as stale as last
        year's model; the mood
                as bleak as life on Mars.

Nonfiction stands for any-
        thing but. Dead men's
                tales are to no avail.

You're free to invent all
        the facts you want, but sooner
                or later, you're bound to fail.

11.

A question best posed while
        strolling through a grove.
                An answer best floated on

the outbound tide. A tyro
        best kept in a tinderbox.
                They say she'll make

a lovely bride. Meanwhile,
        back at the knowledge
                factory, arcane letters

provoke some palaver while
        stepwise melodies with beats
                we can dance to

caress the airwaves night
        and day. But no, Patrón.
                We admit no exceptions.

These are the passions to
        which you aspire. If you want
                the heat, bring the fire.

12.

Having reached the tip
    of the tipping point, we have
        come to the end of an era.

Upright cattails wave in
    the marshes. Loons paddle
        with fluorescent feet. Dawn

breaks on the eastern shore.
    A windless morning becalms
        the water. Where inland

orchards once scented the air. And
    before that, corn and bean fields
        grew. And before that countless

beasts and fowls. And before that
    came Pangaea. Now there are only
        corporate campuses, housing

tracts, and malls. And now
    it remains for the disaffected
        to ask if this is all.

Fire Music

1.

The lives of the elders are unutterably sad, more than anyone could know. After leaving their local at last call, three old cronies head for home. What matters most is securing the terms of a truce that everyone can live with. These were the war years, after all, when the least misrecognition could be fatal. Faith in the cleansing power of truth led to hope for reconciliation, exposing a culture of secrets and lies that could make a tribunal's day. It's a very old story with a global reach. But that's not what we came to say. A brutal sun shone down on the camps, where refugees, long since inured to violence, prayed for better days. This, we were told, is how things would stand until peace broke out among the tribes and the long trek home began.

2.

What did you imagine life would be like for the person who wrote what you've written? And while that's not a trick question, it kills any notion of a better self that does your heavy lifting. Be it said, there's no such beast, and we've got the poems to prove it. The "intimate immensity" of our feelings aside, we will not forsake the palace of memory, albeit some assembly is required. Now, let's clean the reality machine and process the language it offers. Taxonomy says, if you name it, you claim it. Ontogeny says that it's yours for a song. But that person's long since been lost in the traces, and those are all but gone. The Vigil has lasted for years on end. We used to go there with all our friends. Now, however, none can recall why we ever thought it mattered.

3.

Something from nothing leaves noone behind to try to name this tune. First, we adduce the presence of poetry. Then, a whiff of hellfire. Even if exile *were* an option, it all but reeks of privilege. So grab your tuning fork and get to work. Immiseration (by weight, not volume) spurs our disgust with the current regime. Parsing its rhetoric of blood and soil, core samples showcase a soulless waste. Outside El Paso, there's a place called Bliss where everyday life was anything but. And that's not to mention the freedom we lost and the times we could have been having. Our standing orders were to smoke 'em if you've got 'em. So we put plenty weed to the flame. Meanwhile, the message from home was brief: "You have only yourself to blame."

4.

There was much to ponder at the bottom of the shaft, not least the treachery that led us there and the lure of the mineral fact. Fool's gold glittered in the noonday sun. A siren warned of fire in the hole. Hope ran deep the vein would pay. It seemed the mountain had a pulse that mirrored ours that day. We live in the blanks between variations where infinite thought dawns cool and clear. Location is all and YOU ARE HERE. Sunlit days are becoming sparse. Historic traumas are open wounds. House arrest's a farce. Childhood's mandate was sink or swim. Elders thrive on singing hymns. The results of the purges were missing pages. Pages that told of a better clime. When the shaft hit bottom, so did we. Caught together in common time.

5.

Perhaps it isn't for us to say but you might want to annotate these dreams. While few could fathom your departure from the script, none will welcome your return to exile. The culture police are content to ignore you, but they love to drink your Scotch. Just last night, the sheriff looked in. And there by the light of the Beaver Moon, we drank to the genius of the place. It was our duty to tread lightly. It's now our duty to walk away. Even the Party faithful could find nothing averse to say. The presence of ghosts was an inconvenience, but the ghost of presence was pure folly, a kind of metaphoric wonder. Admittedly, after all these years, we'd greet the resurgence of Thing Language. Only that which constitutes an object can hope to warrant its existence.

6.

A ship's bell rang out a round on the house. The resident artist rendered Crusoe bemused by thoughts of home. He'd been too long in The Doldrums and had no urge to roam. Unfed, unsorted, and ill disposed, we've stayed too long ourselves. The subtitle says that we're grammar fluid. But that's neither here not there. History shows there were sound reasons that bebop spoke to modernity. It was largely down to a nurturant tongue. Whence the injunction to bike up the strand. If in the rain, then in the rain. Let childhood's fractions comfort you: two-thirds of three-quarters is just over half-way home. But the rules of this game are strictly ad hoc. To every canopy, its biome. To every poet, her day. If we say that the page *contains* the text, what makes its subject matter?

7.

Hope was faint when peace broke out and the long trek home began. War and famine had scarred the land. A brutal sun shone down on the camps where refugees, long inured to violence, prayed for better days. But that's not what we came to say. In fact, it's the oldest of stories. How faith in the cleansing power of truth led to hope for reconciliation, exposing a culture of secrets and lies that could make a tribunal's day. What mattered most was securing the terms of a truce that everyone could live with. These were the war years, after all, when the least misrecognition could be fatal. Leaving their local at last call, three old cronies head for home. Their days are numbered, and their pace is slow. The lives of the elders are unutterably sad, more than anyone could know.

8.

Tradition dictates that we keep the Vigil. But no one remembers who it's for or why we thought it mattered. Taxonomy says, if you name it, you claim it. Ontogeny says, it's yours for a song. But that person's long since been lost in the traces. And we've grown tired of searching faces. Even so, on rainy days, we stand at reality's door. The "intimate immensity" of our feelings aside, we ponder life in the palace of memory (where some assembly is required). Given what there remains to say – and we have the poems to prove it – there never was a better self to do your heavy lifting. But, the virtues of labor aside, when you first knew you were smitten, what did you imagine life would be like for the person who wrote what you've written?

9.

Outside El Paso, there's a place called Bliss, where life was anything but. Best to elide the time we spent and the life we thought we were missing. Our standing orders were to smoke 'em if you've got 'em, so we did every chance we could. The message from home was "Don't blame me." It's entirely possible for things to go wrong. Lines of demarcation are here and now. Immiseration (by weight, not volume) spurs our disgust with the current regime. Tracing their rhetoric of blood and soil, core samples showcase a soulless waste. Even as exile remains an option, it smacks too much of privilege. So grab your tuning fork and get to work. First, deduct any hint of poetry. Then accept that something from nothing leaves less than nothing to say.

10.

The purges resulted in missing pages – pages that told of a better clime. When the shaft bottomed out, so did we, caught as we were in common time. Childhood's mandate was sink or swim. The elders just tread water. Where historic traumas reopen wounds, house arrest is a farce. Location is everything, and YOU ARE HERE where sunlit days are sparse. We live in the shadow of variations where infinite thought dawns cool and clear. It's as though it had a pulse of its own that mirrored our growing fears. But then what follows an uncertain outcome? A siren warned of fire in the hole. While fool's gold glittered in the noonday sun, there was plenty to ponder at the bottom of the shaft, not least the treachery that led us there and the lure of the mineral fact.

11.

Only that which constitutes an object can hope to warrant its existence. Even or especially after all these years, we welcome the return of Thing Language. Though the ghost of presence is pure folly, the presence of ghosts is increasingly common and not to be dismissed. Even the party faithful were surprised. It was then our duty to tread lightly. It's now our duty to walk away. Last night, under a Beaver Moon, we drank to the morbid genius of the place. The culture police are content to ignore you, but they love to drink your Scotch. Much like your poems, it's an acquired taste. Where few could fathom your departure from the script, none will welcome your return to exile. Perhaps it isn't for us to say, but you might want to annotate your dreams.

12.

If we say the page *contains* the text, what makes its subject matter? To every canopy, its biome. To every poet, her day. The rules are neither hard not fast. And most are of your own devising. Two thirds of three-quarters is just over halfway home. Whence the injunction to bike up the strand. If in the rain, then in the rain. History shows there were sound reasons that bebop spoke to modernity. But don't let that disturb you. It's down to a nurturant tongue. The marquee says that we're grammar fluid. Unfed, unsorted, and ill disposed, we've been too long in The Doldrums. Stay here long enough and you lose the urge to roam. When a ship's bell rang out a round on the house, the resident artist rendered Crusoe bemused by thoughts of home.

Equinox

Equinox

1.

Born in Arcadia

        to lyric weather.

"As for subsistence,

        'No thanks.'"

    Whose voice is

        tidal in its ebbs

      and flows. Whose eyes

          tell all she knows.

Our elders

    taught us right

  from wrong. But

      not how to

    tell the singer

        from her song.

2.

Whose head is his

    homeland has

shelved his psalms –

    which are

no match for

    the overamped

blasts that scour the

    streets by day.

Painfully clear to

    all who can hear,

this isn't an issue

    of protected speech

but of one more

    unsure egoist.

3.

Whose roots run

        deeper than

    the deepest hell

           through which all

        words must pass.

                Without medi-

          ation, there can

                  be no polity.

Where exile

        beckons like a

    false prophet,

        the book has

        been described

            as a tomb.

4.

Lay down your burden

        is sound advice. Memory

stirs and is bestirred.

        A word called lichen

blooms on surfaces.

        Love in vain is a

long story, unless

        it's not all pain.

While studio guests

        played What's My Line?,

the unknown subject

        lost track of time.

When he was born, the

        subway was a dime.

5.

Implied pulses underscore

        pitch events. Every other

    shot is an angel's portion.

          A minute describes

    a heart's beat. Wherever one

            thing leads to another,

       melody follows where

              its rhythms lead.

The blank page mirrors

    a tabula rasa. Code

emerges where words

      are spent. Whose diction

    tempers common speech.

          Another pitch event.

6.

A hushed ascent has

    bagged a summit. Passwords

alter when spoken

    aloud. A bridge too

far has flummoxed the

    drummer, but he'll

recover, unbent and

    unbowed. Meanwhile,

we're waiting on

    diminishing returns as

forests burn and oceans rise.

    Add in famine and a

global plague and it's

    far from Paradise.

7.

Deep in the dusk of our

        metaphoric day, years

    of cadenzas followed

        decades of pauses. Back

    drafts of cherished

          fragments lay in ashes

    on the studio

          floor. Star shine

vied with light pollution.

    The road home followed

  the path of shadows, which

    is where we spent

  our final days, dodging

        the Hunter's Moon.

8.

Trained off leash to

        accommodate contingency,

we're on the hook for

        what comes next. A

    string of words, as dense

            as matter, forms

        the border of a

                legendary realm

whose outline gets us

        home by feel. Empty

of content and sworn

        to silence, nothing

speaks truth like a

            lapse in the Real.

9.

Best to follow the

        protocols of spring,

    where blossoms wait

          on the last frost, and

      early summer brings

             skies of gray. This

        is the fabled marine

                layer, which

a friend has rendered

      in poems that abide.

    But first, to survive

          the current plague

      with my rider

            by my side.

10.

Let's raise a glass to

                the excluded middle.

To that which is neither

                fair nor foul. For

there lies the ictus

                of the rictus rictus,

        where we loaded

                          our riffs with lore.

Riffs which, parsed,

        foretold our demise

as we looked to the future

        with hungry eyes and

followed the arc and

                the roll of the dice.

11.

The pianist broods

        upon his bench while

    the horns interweave

           their lines, stringing to-

        gether riffs he's heard –

           far too many times.

        Hence, his search

                  for newer noises

tuned to the variable

        rhythms of his days.

     He plies the keys from

        dusk to dawn in

     search of the outermost

           limits of song.

12.

May these lyrics weather

        whatever life brings. *To*

    the moment. *On* the beat.

            As red-lined decibels

      flog the street, memory

            yearns for a muted

        horn whose contours

                  limn the air we breathe.

And though such memories

      give you pause, don't

    let the future catch you

        napping. (A fading tremolo

      ends the set to the sound

            of one hand clapping.)

Codices

1.

An impossible figure plagues my sleep. Who is the patron saint of abjection? What keeps old souls up after hours? What began *that* which ended *away*? When measure went looking for the pulse of thought, did the high road hum with singularities? To get off meant to get it on. So the lovers went all in. The cave mouth bid the buyer beware of password envy if he tarry there. The increase in victims was exponential. The plague of laughter was not without menace. I remember pictures of falling angels. I forget from whence they came. But they only confirm what experience teaches, that hard times can always get harder. The form of the sentence, which can say no more, obliges me to stay. That, and the rapidly fading hope that "the sun is gonna shine in my back door some day."

2.

It might be art, but it's not divination. Your best guess is as good as mine. Some days maybe better. But whoever said it can't hurt to try has never played this town. Where Brutalist blocks of cold-water flats ran all too true to form, we had one lightbulb to keep us warm. When they said the poor would always be with us, they forgot to mention we were poor. No mere oversight. Rest assured. We were left to rely on our own devices. Where barred windows signified street-level living, peddlers vied with buskers for scraps. Then, on the *n*+seventh day, Art awoke to a buzz. Now, we ponder the weather from the heights. Speech acts are awkward at safe distances. And, though we know where we want to be, we don't know how to get there.

3.

I'm not inclined to spell it out when you could look it up. Whose questions can be answered with their own words. Whose works span crumbling empires and genres. Whose crystalline structures refract the light. But between your urges and your disquisitions, is there anything left for us? Among constituent pitches and tempos, exactly rendered if barely sustained, there is no plot, implied or not. And what should we make of that? Behind closed doors, the hours pass while poppies lean on forget-me-nots to let us rest at ease. Thus, to the vigilant fall the crumbs. These are they, but which is which? The lyric function is to formalize affect. That tune in your head is solid gold. Others do what others will, but, there's nothing like a stick of tea to keep a body chill.

4.

From the spark of desire to its denouement, you have made your case for parole. Veins of quartz bleed pure crystals. Wind caves sing granite eyes to sleep. They might be sculptures of frozen speech. Or a frieze of memories just out of reach. Natural sounds seek alphabets that serve a common cause. Straight, no chaser, means it's time for cocktails. A change in tempo gives the dancers pause. What stops for a glance stays tuned to a sway. Propriety pales as the jukebox wails and you take Miss Becky by the hand. Where duration lasts beyond all counting, kisses are complicit with the perfumed night. Snapshots fade and then grow brittle. To historicize our trauma avails us little. We, who sit here with our heads in our hands. Chanting: *if so, then.*

5.

Solid time makes for sound practice. Remember to vamp till you get to the bridge. From breath to breeze by way of song, adagios paced us all day long. We struggled for hours over broken shale. Then retired to our local for a pint of ale. There's no need for small talk. We're here to do some drinking. Not for nothing, but the death of tyrants is the object of all our thinking. Exposed rock weathers in the fullness of time. As oceans rise we deem it wise to establish beachheads in the high desert. Our heirs will sail on inland seas as our artifacts settle into submarine strata and sepia hills set a western backdrop where tourists pan for gold. Our future resembles a standing wave, but easy living is our one desire for a species intent on digging its grave.

6.

Albeit we've come to a bedrock moment, there are darker days ahead. It is the asymmetries that stand out most, or will as this puzzle unravels. Hymns to reason use burnished vowels to mellow its glacial idioms. Still bringing heat in the late innings, a former lover puts you in your place. Passing tones lead to deceptive cadences. Absolute zero is rightly invariant. It's all in the changes and how you play them. Because if you do, you're a living fossil. But, if you could, you'd know where you've been. Rose-gold lacquer adorns the horns. Rivets sizzle on beaten brass. Cymbals mark the sting of time. First thought, worst thought. It stands to reason. Irony's never out of season. Who but a friend would sing your praises while consigning your songs to uncut pages?

7.

Sleep itself is an impossible figure. To dream might be art, but it's not divination. Nor am I inclined to spell it out when you could look it up. From the spark of desire to its denouement, you've made a case for parole. Solid time requires sound practice. And though we've arrived at a bedrock moment, there are darker days to come. Whose questions are answered with their own words says veins of quartz bleed pure crystals. So remember to vamp till you get to the bridge. It is the asymmetries that stand out most, or will as this puzzle unravels. Who is the patron saint of abjection? Your best guess is as good as mine. From first breath to last by way of song, this figure plagues me all night long. Whose works span crumbling empires and genres where wind caves sing granite eyes to sleep.

8.

Hymns to reason use burnished vowels to mellow its glacial idioms. What keeps old souls out after hours? Where crystalline structures refract the light, they might be sculptures of frozen speech. Where what began that has ended away, it's slow going over broken shale. Still bringing heat in the late innings, a former lover put you in your place. Where Brutalist flats ran true to form, a single lightbulb kept us warm. Age is but a travesty of what we know of time. And the proper cure for a hard day's thirst begins with tequila and lime. The maestro says that timbre's more than icing on the pitch. Passing tones flirt with deceptive cadences. Resolution is hit or miss. When measure went looking for the pulse of thought, the high road hummed with singularities.

9.

When they said that the poor would always be with us, they forgot to mention we were poor. Among constituent pitches and tempos, exactly rendered if barely sustained, there is no plot, implied or not. Which, rest assured, was no mere oversight. Natural sounds seek alphabets that serve a common cause. It's all in the changes and how you play them, if you ever do. To get off meant to get it on. And what shall we make of that? They say, to the vigilant fall the crumbs. Straight, no chaser, means it's time for cocktails. Now raise a glass to the death of tyrants. It's time for some heavy drinking. Later for tales of love gone wrong and any heavy thinking. Up on the stand, a star is born. Rose-gold lacquer adorns his horn. His notes are true; his tone is warm.

10.

A change in tempo gives the dancers pause. Exposed rock weathers in the fullness of time. The cave mouth bid the buyer beware of password envy if he linger there. Where barred windows signify street level, peddlers vie with buskers for scraps. Hours pass behind closed doors while poppies lean on forget-me-nots to let us take our ease. What stops for a glance stays tuned to a sway. As oceans rise we deem it wise to establish beachheads in the high desert. When rivets sizzle on beaten brass, cymbals mark the sting of time. The increase in victims is exponential. These are they, but which is which? Then, on the n+seventh day, Art awoke to the kind of buzz from which all blessings flow.

11.

Our heirs will sail on inland seas. The plague of laughter is not without menace. We ponder the daily weather from the heights. The lyric function is to formalize affect. As duration lasts beyond all counting, kisses are complicit with the perfumed night. Artifacts will settle in submarine strata. I remember pictures of falling angels. I forget from whence they came. Speech acts are awkward at safe distances, but the tune in your head is solid gold. Sepia hills set a western motif. When your first thought's your worst thought, it stands to reason that you would pursue your prey out of season. You've made your case for the Grail quite clear. We regret you can't get there from here.

12.

Others do what others will. But there's nothing like a stick of tea to keep you feeling chill. Tourists are happy to pan for gold, but digging for trauma requires better tools. Which only adds to your old suspicion that words are "the currency of fools." Given, that age is a travesty of what we know of time. Thus, to confirm what experience teaches: bad luck worsens as you go down the line. Now for some tales of love gone wrong. We're tired of heavy thinking. We'd trade our kingdom for some down-home blues and a dedicated night of drinking. Let's raise a glass to the death of tyrants. It was only a matter of where and when. Whatever comes next is beyond our ken. So you sit here, head in hands, chanting your mantra – *if so, then.*

Matchsticks

1.

Introvert life is benchmarked by defeats.
The odds on beating the house are nil.

Where right angles mock your perpetual drift,
Miracles speak to your sense of the absurd.

We've come to the end of another era.
Alexa! Use meretricious in a sentence.

It's hard to survive your expectations when
Language affords you no shelter to speak of.

The culture police have closed the borders.
Who will mourn the wild child's fate?

While the search goes on for your lost libido,
Your memory essays your reckless past.

2.

Lust isn't love, but it has its charms
As lovers attest in each others' arms.

Twilight finds you lost in the pharmakon.
Let's count the ways you could hit bottom.

Obvious to remark, we are mostly water.
Childhood's mandate was sink or swim.

What can't be named will not be tamed.
The oracles agree. It's all in your head.

Let there be no talk of resurrection.
Each next poem might be your last.

Your morning labors leave you spent,
But "the tide comes in twice a day."

3.

The *pass* completes your formal education.
You have wrapped your troubles in dreams.

As the last in a series of historical asides,
Nothing comes of standing by your word.

By factors so vast you seek an abridgement,
The City of Ciphers explodes into view.

The sanctuary opens on a stairway to the stars.
From there, it's only seven steps to heaven.

The current regime has silenced your song
With anthems of blood and soil.

Whence you descend and resume your life
Among people "incapable of contact."

4.

With the casual grace of a practiced dancer,
You tender your mercies and your resignation.

In a life spent milking blood from a stone,
Your blind side faces wherever you turn.

Chalk it up to a bad case of nerves. You live
In the shadow of the sum of your parts.

Once you've gathered your bushel of doubt,
To be quit with offers a kind of consolation.

When totality beckons, fangs and all,
You barely escape The Big Picture.

But as long as the Grail remains at large,
Its legend will secure your existence.

5.

Subjects flow from the subject factory.
Desire spirals from disaster to disaster.

Evidence of thought is missing in action.
Chronic fantasies supplant your dreams.

Fantasies of place, in which you have one.
Fantasies of time, in which you survive.

Exiled, you pass through uncharted waters.
At sunset, you turn your back on the sea.

Where life exacts a succession of failures,
Reality appears as a kind of delirium.

Sleep evades you, but not these voices,
Which linger like uninvited guests.

6.

"The object *is*. Now what objects *aren't*?"
Do we write just to fill these pages?

Dead silence greeted your latest recital.
Heartbreak followed you into the street.

Imaginary lightning illumines your path
As if you were not (and are not) alone.

Other voices tell other lies. Finding yourself
At a loss for words should come as no surprise.

When heavy weather approached the city,
Rolling thunder wasn't far behind.

The object in question speaks for itself.
You speak at peril if you speak your mind.

7.

Right angles mock your perpetual drift.
Miracles speak to your sense of the absurd.

It's hard to survive your expectations when
Language affords you no shelter to speak of.

While the search goes on for your lost libido,
Your memory essays your reckless past.

Introvert life is benchmarked by defeats.
The odds on beating the house are nil.

We have come to the end of another era.
Alexa! Use meretricious in a sentence.

The culture police have closed the borders.
Who will mourn the wild child's fate?

8.

Twilight finds you lost in the pharmakon.
Let's count the ways to hit bottom.

What can't be named will not be tamed.
The oracles agree. It's all in your head.

Let there be no talk of resurrection.
Each next poem might be your last.

Lust isn't love, but it has its charms
As lovers attest in each others' arms.

Obvious to remark, we are mostly water.
Childhood's mandate was sink or swim.

Your morning labors leave you spent,
But "the tide comes in twice a day."

9.

After the deluge, you resume your life
Among people "incapable of contact."

In the last in a series of historical asides,
Nothing comes of standing by your word.

Now that you've wrapped your troubles in dreams,
Your dreams have turned into nightmares.

By factors so vast you seek an abridgement,
the City of Ciphers explodes into view.

The current regime has silenced your song
With anthems of blood and soil.

The sanctuary opens on a stairway to the stars.
From there, it's seven steps to heaven.

10.

Once you've gathered your bushel of doubt,
To be quit with offers a kind of consolation.

When totality beckons, fangs and all,
You barely escape The Big Picture.

But as long as the Grail remains at large,
Its legend will secure your existence.

With the casual grace of a practiced dancer,
You tender your mercies and your resignation.

In a life spent milking blood from a stone,
Your blind side faces wherever you turn.

Chalk it up to a bad case of nerves. You live
In the shadow of the sum of your parts.

11.

Where life exacts a succession of failures,
Reality appears as a kind of delirium –

From fantasies of place, in which you have one,
To fantasies of time, in which you survive.

Sleep evades you, but not these voices,
Which linger like uninvited guests.

Subjects flow from the subject factory.
Desire spirals from disaster to disaster.

Evidence of thought is missing in action.
Chronic fantasies supplant your dreams.

Exiled, you pass through uncharted waters.
At sunset, you turn your back on the sea.

12.

"The object *is*. Now what objects *aren't*?"
Do we write just to fill these pages?

Other voices tell other lies. Finding yourself
At a loss for words should come as no surprise.

When heavy weather approaches the city,
Rolling thunder isn't far behind.

The object in question speaks for itself.
You speak at peril if you speak your mind.

Dead silence greeted your latest recital.
Heartbreak followed you into the street.

Imaginary lightning illumines your path
As if you were not (and are not) alone.

TED PEARSON was born and raised in Palo Alto, California. He began writing poetry in 1964 and subsequently attended Vandercook College of Music, Foothill College, and San Francisco State. His first book, *The Grit*, appeared in 1976. He has since published twenty-five books of poetry, including *Extant Glyphs 1964-1980* (2014), *An Intermittent Music 1975-2010* (2016) and his most recent, *Last Date* (2020). He also co-authored *The Grand Piano,* a ten-volume experiment in collective autobiography. He now lives in Houston, Texas.